TALKING
ABOUT
BOOKS

A STEP-BY-STEP GUIDE
FOR PARTICIPATING IN A
BOOK DISCUSSION GROUP

MARCIA FINEMAN, PH.D.

*Thank you to Betsy, Jane and Jennifer who each gave me a
different kind of feedback, no matter how many times I asked.*

*Thank you to Joanne and my book club friends who were willing
to try out the questions and the planning sheets during our book club discussions.*

*Thank you to my kind friend Charlotte who spurred me on to look at things
one more time every time I thought it was the very last time.*

*A special thank you to Jonas. May all of his great ideas for the
future of this guide come true.*

**TALKING
ABOUT
BOOKS**

P. O. Box 10202
Rockville, MD 20849
USA
**301-913-0353
800-484-7594 #7586**
TalkBook@aol.com

Talking About Books: A Step-by-Step Guide for Participating in a Book Discussion Group
ISBN 0-9661567-0-6

First Edition.

Cover illustration and book design by Carole L. Skog McGeehan, Big IF Studio, Wheaton, MD.

TABLE OF CONTENTS

WHY *TALKING ABOUT BOOKS* IS FOR YOU

*T*alking About Books offers both old and new book discussion groups a remarkably easy and enjoyable guide to creating exhilarating discussions about fiction and biographies. Simply organized and easy to use, *Talking About Books* first describes what happens in a book discussion group, then defines the five literary characteristics of a novel and its theme, and offers suggestions about how to talk about each of these points.

The section entitled **"Suggested Questions to Ask When Talking About Books"** lists discussion questions for each of the characteristics of a novel and reproducible **"Discussion Planning Sheets"** are provided for the facilitator and group members to use to record selected questions for each specific discussion.

The section entitled **"Guidelines for Book Discussion Meetings"** is especially useful for those who would like to form a book club, or are in the process of forming one. *Talking About Books* is such a valuable resource that each group member will be eager to have a copy of their own.

Talking About Books answers the following questions asked by all book discussion group members:

1 What happens during a book discussion group meeting?

2 What are the five characteristics of a novel and what do group members need to know about them in order to discuss their books in depth?

3 What are some questions that will lead readers to in-depth discussions, personal insights and new knowledge when talking about a novel?

4 How can existing book discussion groups get more out of their discussions?

5 What are easy procedures for planning and maintaining a new book discussion group?

TALKING ABOUT BOOKS

Have you ever finished reading a book and wanted to talk with someone about what you had read? Have you ever had the desire to share your feelings about a character that you met in a novel with someone who also had come to know that person? Have you ever disagreed with the way a problem was solved in a story and wished that you could tell someone how you would have behaved in the same situation?

I have!

INTRODUCTION

Over the past 35 years, I have studied and taught reading to children and adults. During this time I also have had the great pleasure of participating in a variety of book discussion groups. It always has been exciting and interesting to discuss my reactions with others and to explore questions and uncertainties I've had about books I've read. Some groups were made up of close friends who had come together to talk about, among many other things, a book we had all read. Other groups were formed for the sole purpose of talking about books. One of the most interesting and memorable discussion groups I belonged to was with beginning reading adults who had never had the opportunity to discuss books before.

Each group developed a personality of its own. Often, in the beginning, members didn't know how to get a discussion going, what questions to ask, or what to talk about. Some discussions focused on the events in the story and on sharing opinions about the quality of the book. In other groups, individuals wanted to share more about themselves and the personal connections they had made with the characters and situations in the novels.

Over time, I realized that the most successful and enjoyable book discussion groups for me were those where all members used the same reading language when we were discussing books. In these groups, members agreed and disagreed during discussions, but when everyone understood the characteristics of a novel in the same way, the discussions were more focused, more stimulating and more profound. In these groups, members often expressed satisfaction about what they took away from the discussion.

Book discussion groups are becoming more and more popular. Colleagues and friends that know of my work in reading and know how fond I am of belonging to book discussion groups often ask me about how to get a group started and how to keep it going. They also often ask me to suggest questions and topics for discussions.

This step-by-step guide was written to help people interested in beginning a book discussion group get started, and for groups that already exist to extend and refine their discussions. I hope that this guide will support stimulating book discussion groups.

THE PURPOSE OF
TALKING ABOUT BOOKS

Talking *About Books* is designed for book discussion group members to use in four ways:

1 To become aware of what happens during a book discussion group.

Book discussion groups may be different from what many people remember from early school reading experiences. This guide describes what happens in a book discussion when all members share opinions and explore insights into both the content and the characters of a novel.

2 To understand the five characteristics — Setting, Characterization, Plot, Conflict/Resolution, Character Motivation — and Theme of a novel.

When group members have a common understanding of the characteristics of a novel and use this understanding as they talk about books, each member is able to discuss the story in the same way. This guide provides group members with the language of books that leads to in-depth and interesting discussions.

3 To plan for discussions by providing suggested discussion questions and sample discussion planning sheets.

Every book is different and, therefore, can be discussed in a different way. The suggested discussion questions provided for each characteristic of a novel can be used to help facilitators and group members plan for discussions. Discussions might be planned to focus on all or just some of the literary characteristics, as well as on the variety of personal connections that different readers bring to a text.

4 To maintain a successful book discussion group.

Groups are more interesting and fun when all members agree from the beginning on the logistics of getting together, the roles that participants will play, the ground rules for discussions, and the procedures for how to decide upon which book to discuss. This guide will help groups decide upon which procedures to implement that will best fit the group's needs.

What Happens During a Book Discussion Group Meeting?

The members of a book discussion group come together to talk about a book that everyone in the group has read. Groups can discuss fiction, non-fiction or a combination of the two. This guide is designed for groups that discuss **fiction**, specifically **novels** and **biographies**. (Even though biographies are considered non-fiction, they have the same characteristics as novels and can be discussed in the same way.)

An author is an artist who uses words instead of drawings to create images. Readers use the images to form mental pictures of the characters and the places and times in which the characters in a novel live and function.

In a novel, an author tries to present understandable people who experience life in realistic settings. The author hopes that each reader will be provided with enough information to make connections with the characters' personalities and behaviors, and the ways the characters solve their problems and resolve their conflicts. However, an author can only include a limited amount of information in a novel.

Even though everyone in a book discussion group has read the **same** novel, each individual's understanding is based on prior knowledge, background of experience, and personal reactions to the characters, events and decisions the characters make. As a result, readers often make different connections and draw different conclusions about the same book. Unless the author of a novel is available to answer clarifying questions or to provide additional information, readers have to discern meaning for themselves. The different understandings, connections and interpretations of a novel are what make book discussion groups so exciting.

During a book discussion, members focus on a variety of topics. Sometimes people talk about content that is unfamiliar or controversial. Sometimes discussions relate to topics about which readers already have strong opinions. Book characters behave in interesting and curious ways and readers often talk about how they would have behaved similarly or differently from the ways characters react to life situations, events and experiences.

Book discussions often are most interesting and thought provoking when group members do not agree. When a group of people read and discuss the same novel, there are bound to be different points of view and attitudes about the characters, the content and the quality of the text. It is always important to remember that no matter how strongly individuals state personal opinions, there really are no "**right**" or "**wrong**" ideas when it comes to talking about books.

At a book discussion, readers come together to analyze characters and to share perceptions, opinions and reactions to the events in a novel. Participants discuss why characters behave the ways they do and hypothesize about what an author may have wanted readers to learn. Group members attempt to validate perceptions by discussing personal reactions to the characters' behaviors and to the events that occur. Participants share opinions about the ideas and issues presented and about the quality of the novel by sharing reactions and inter-pretations and by providing support for those interpretations. Discussions often lead group members to new insights and understandings of the novel and of life in general.

In a successful book discussion, participants continuously strive to establish and maintain an accepting and non-threatening climate where every individual feels encouraged to contribute, to ask clarifying questions and to offer personal reactions related to the novel under consideration. Group members need to listen to one another carefully and to suspend judgments about what others say until they understand the different points of view that are presented.

THE FIVE CHARACTERISTICS AND THEME OF A NOVEL

Every piece of fiction — every story — has five specific literary characteristics: Setting, Characterization, Plot, Conflict/Resolution, and Character Motivation. Theme also is important.

When group participants have a common understanding of the five characteristics of a novel and know how to identify the theme, they can discuss a novel together more clearly and in more depth.

AND

HOW TO TALK ABOUT THEM

The Five Characteristics and Theme of a Novel

1 **Setting.**
The time and the place in which the story occurs.

2 **Characterization.**
A character's traits, feelings and attitudes.

3 **Plot.**
The main events; and the causes and effects of those events.

4 **Conflict/Resolution.**
The major conflict the main character faces and the decision that is made to resolve the character's conflict.

5 **Character Motivation.**
The reasons characters behave in the ways they do.

Theme.
Lessons or universal truths gained about the world and human experience presented through the content of a story.

CHARACTERISTIC: SETTING

Setting concerns time and place and if and how time and place affected the characters, the events and the decisions that the characters made.

The **setting** of a novel includes **both the place where** and the **time when** the events in a story occur. An author provides both specific information and inferential clues to the setting by including objects, customs, references to real people and real events and descriptions that are consistent with specific places and times. Novels generally include multiple settings. Chapters serve the purpose of changing the place or indicating the passage of time, or both.

1 **Place.**
Place refers to the **location** or locations where the events in the story occur. Place can be set in any, or in a combination of any, of the following:
- a geographical region — desert, forest, mountain, island, plain;
- a specific country, state or city — Spain, New York, Miami;
- a type of community — city, suburb, rural area, inner city;
- a type of building — school, grocery store, office, house; and/or
- a type of vehicle — space ship, boat, covered wagon, car.

In some novels, the place does not change. **For example, the actions in an entire novel might be set in one house. A different novel might take place on a ship in the middle of an ocean.** Generally, a novel is set in a variety of locations. **One chapter might take place in New York City, the next in a hospital room in a small town in Connecticut and another in the bedroom of the main character's home on Long Island.** The setting in this novel could be described as taking place in several states in the eastern United States.

2 **Time.**
Time refers to the **period** or periods when the events in the story happen. Time can be set in any, or in a combination of any, of the following:
- a season — Summer, Fall, Winter, Spring;
- a time of day — dawn, morning, afternoon, night;
- a time span — past, present, future;
- a holiday — Christmas, Halloween, Passover;
- a specific period — Civil War, the 1920s, Middle Ages; and/or
- a specific day, year or date — 1776, 1929, December 7, 1941.

In some novels, the time does not change. **All of the actions in one novel might occur during one afternoon on July 4, 1776, or during an afternoon**

wedding celebration in 2005. Generally, novels occur over a period of time. **One chapter might take place on a summer evening in 1912, the next at dawn several years later, and another on a specific date in the following year.** The setting in this novel could be described as taking place during the early 1900s.

3 **Effect of Setting on Characters.**
At some level, setting always affects characters. Individuals living in different places, during different time periods are influenced by the people, ideas and objects that exist around them. **The effect of setting on characters living in an Italian village during the Middle Ages is different from the effect on those living in a modern Italian village. Living on a farm in China during the reign of the first emperor is different from living on a farm in China during the Cultural Revolution or in 1997.**

In some novels, the setting does not play a major role. In these novels, the stories could take place anywhere, at any time. The setting in these novels does not have a major impact on the characters' behaviors or on their actions, but merely provides a backdrop for the events to occur in the story. **For example, a novel might take place during the winter in a small French town,** but the season and the location may have little significance to the events that occur.

Setting has a **major effect** on characters when it has an impact on the way they behave. In these novels, the events that occur and the decisions that are made could only happen in that specific place or at that particular time. **For example, a novel might take place on a farm in a small German town in 1943. A character's decision about whether or not to protect a friend may be based on possible danger to his/her family because of the situation occurring in Germany at that time.** Time also can affect characters. **For example, a story might take place during a winter storm on a mountain when a character has to decide whether or not he/she has the courage to face the elements, despite risk and great personal danger, in order to save a friend.**

In novels where setting plays a major role, sometimes there is not a strong story line. In this type of novel, the setting may take on a character of its own.

TALKING ABOUT SETTING

First, identify the setting of the story. Talk about whether or not the author created a consistent image of place and time so that the reader could understand the actions and events in the story.

Some readers may have lived in or visited the places in which the story is set. Share how the author's representation compares with the reader's recollection. When readers are not familiar with the places, discuss what the group learned while reading about this new location.

When novels are set in time periods that members have not experienced, past or future, discuss insights about the effect of time. When readers do not have direct experiences with a setting, they might also share other books they have read that were set in the same place and time as the novel under consideration.

Readers often hypothesize about how characters might have behaved had they lived in other places or times. Explore perceptions about whether or not the setting affected the characters' actions and choices. Predict how the characters might behave if they lived in different settings.

The place and time in which the author of a novel lived, matured and wrote is also valuable to consider. Discuss whether the characters appear to be influenced by the life experiences of the author, and, if so, in what way. **For example, if an author, born and raised in the North, wrote a novel set in the South, discuss whether the author's background affected the characters' behaviors or the events in the story, and in what way.**

Some authors use language dramatically, figuratively, descriptively and/or poetically to create vivid word pictures. Readers often are able to imagine the characters living in the specific place and time. Share scenes that readers particularly enjoyed and specific images of the setting that touched them positively or negatively. Identify scenes from the novel where readers feel that the author might have gone into more or less detail and discuss reasons for readers' reactions. Discuss if the author's skill in describing the setting enhanced or detracted from the novel.

SEE PAGE 26 FOR SUGGESTED DISCUSSION QUESTIONS ABOUT SETTING.

CHARACTERISTIC: CHARACTERIZATION

Characterization concerns each character's traits, feelings and attitudes and whether or not a character changed as a result of what he/she learned or experienced.

Because more than one character often plays a key role in a novel, different readers may differ in their choice of who the main character is. The **main character** generally is the individual who, throughout the story, consistently faces challenging problems and, eventually, has a conflict to resolve. The role played by other significant characters and by minor characters is to reveal more about the main character and to provide readers with information about the main character's traits, feelings and attitudes in order to explain the main character's behaviors, decisions and motivation. Not all characters are fully developed in every novel, but the main character is so that readers can understand that character's decisions.

1 **Character Traits.**
A character **trait** is a consistent **behavior** or **quality** that an individual exhibits over time, often over a lifetime. All people exhibit a variety of traits. **For example, everyone is generous at some time or other, but not all people would be described as generous. A person is described as generous when he/she exhibits consistent**

actions over time that illustrate the trait of generosity. Other traits that could describe a character are: curious, honest, arrogant, intelligent, cruel, thoughtful, humorous, irresponsible, etc.

Readers identify a character's traits from behaviors, conversations and thoughts and from the ways the character interacts with others. The more consistent examples that an author includes to illustrate a character's traits, the better readers are able to understand a character and to identify the type of person that character represents.

Characters in a novel are multidimensional; they exhibit more than one trait in the same story. **An author might portray a character as honest, kind, creative and lazy; another character might be intelligent, generous and cruel.** Minor characters and other significant characters frequently possess traits that enhance those of the main character.

In novels, as in real life, traits last a long time and are difficult to change. When a character does change, the change is often the result of living through a significant experience and/or an important interaction with events, situations and/or other people. When the main character changes, generally only one trait is affected. **For example, a curious, fun-loving, irresponsible person may witness the death or illness of a** family member, meet a person who makes a significant impact on him/her or experience a reversal of fortune. As a result, an irresponsible character may become hard-working and responsible.

2 Character Feelings.
Feelings are the same as **emotions**. Feelings are often short lived and frequently change from moment to moment (unlike traits that last over a long period of time). Feelings are dependent on the events, experiences and situations that occur. Readers understand a character's feelings when they determine the reasons for the feelings from the interactions and the events that happen in the story.

A character who is identified as having a particular trait can experience a wide range of feelings. **For example, a person described as happy and upbeat can feel sad because a friend has died. A character identified as pessimistic and sour can feel pleasure because he/she finally has been recognized for an accomplishment.** Identifying the characters' feelings and the reasons for the feelings help readers better understand the characters and their choices.

3 Character Attitudes.
An attitude is an **opinion** or point of view that an individual has toward a specific topic, group or issue. Attitudes develop as a result of geography, education, family background, economics, culture, age, etc. Attitudes are described as positive, neutral or negative. **As a result of growing up in a large happy family, a character might have**

a positive attitude toward having children. Conversely, as a result of coming from a large unhappy family where money was a difficult issue and everyone had to do without, a character might have a negative attitude toward having children.

Authors help readers identify and understand a character's attitudes by providing consistent actions, dialogue and thoughts that the character has about specific topics. Authors often use change or resistance to change to convey an opinion or to bring attention to specific messages they want readers to understand.

4 Character Change.
Main characters often **change a trait or an attitude** toward a person, object, issue or event. **A character with a negative attitude toward children might learn from an experience with a friend's family that children can play positive roles.**

Sometimes a character may show an unwillingness to change or compromise a strongly held opinion. Readers can see a change in traits and attitudes when characters make or think about making major decisions that reflect new reactions or surprising choices related to an individual, object, issue or event. In some novels, characters do not change. They continue to make decisions that reflect the strength of their opinions and reveal that they are unwilling to compromise or consider new ideas despite the consequences. Whether or not a character changes, an author may focus on change to highlight or reinforce a topic important to the writer.

Talking About Characterization

First, identify the main character and other significant characters. Talk about why a particular character was chosen as the main character and support the choice with information from the novel.

1 Identify the characters' traits.

Discussions are especially interesting when readers differ about the choice of the main character and give support for their selection with specific evidence from the story.

Discuss whether the author presented a consistent, realistic portrayal of each character's **traits** by citing examples of actions and dialogue to illustrate each identified trait. The more consistently an author provides clear examples of actions and dialogue, the easier it is for readers to identify the types of people the characters are meant to portray.

Talk about whether or not a character changes and identify the events and experiences that contributed to the change. If a character did not change or was not willing to compromise, discuss why no change seemed to occur.

2 Identify the characters' feelings.

Talk about whether or not a character's reactions to people and events were realistic and justifiable. Discuss the similarities and differences between a character's and the reader's feelings about the people, events, situations and experiences encountered in the novel. Share opinions about which feelings seemed to influence a character's decisions.

3 Identify characters' attitudes and the reasons for those attitudes.

A novelist often presents a message or a point of view about a specific topic, person, group or issue. Talk about how the author's attitude toward a topic is revealed through one or more character's behaviors, thoughts and feelings.

After identifying an attitude, discuss the similarities and differences between a character's and the author's attitude toward the same topic. Share opinions about how effectively the author presented a character's attitude about a topic and give possible reasons about why the author presented the message that way. Have readers share their attitudes toward the same topic and discuss how readers' attitudes are the same or different from those of the characters in the story.

Readers often admire or dislike the characters they meet in novels. Share which characters each reader connected with and which characters each reader did or did not admire. Give personal insights about what readers learned from the behaviors, feelings and attitudes of the characters in the novel.

SEE PAGE 27 FOR SUGGESTED DISCUSSION QUESTIONS ABOUT CHARACTERIZATION.

CHARACTERISTIC: PLOT

Plot concerns the main events and the causes and effects of the events.

1 Main Events.

The **plot** of a novel is the **story line**, the **framework**, the **structure** of the story. A novelist reveals the plot through the events that occur in the story. **Main events** are the significant experiences or important situations the characters live through. Main events help readers understand the characters' problems and the decisions they make about how to resolve the conflict that will occur late in the novel.

Throughout a novel an author presents events that provide readers with information. An event is considered to be significant to the story line when it leads the main character to new insights, to the need to act or make a choice, to a change, or when the character must make a decision. Some examples of main events that frequently occur in novels are situations where characters:

- face a challenge, difficulty or tragedy;
- experience a success or triumph;
- participate in a situation for the first time;
- meet someone for the first time;
- live through an historic event;
- come to a conclusion about a person, object or idea;
- gain a personal insight; and/or
- discover something about other characters.

When there are several important characters in a novel, readers identify and analyze the main events in relation to the impact they have on the main character. The events in which other characters participate — the subplots — contribute to helping readers better understand the main character.

2 Cause.

The **reason** a main event occurs is the **cause**. Each main event can have single or multiple causes. When a main event occurs, readers can look back in the text to identify the information the author included as the cause of the event.

3 Effect.

The **result** of a main event is the **effect**. The effect of a main event generally moves the plot of the novel forward because the outcome of one event is often the cause of another. The effect of a main event frequently leads to change. Examples of outcomes frequently found in novels that lead to change include changes in:

- a physical location;
- a relationship;
- a way of behaving or feeling;
- attitude; and/or
- life becoming easier or more difficult.

Sometimes an outcome of an event may be that no change occurs. When no change occurs, the event may serve to explain why a character maintains a position.

Main events can have single or multiple causes and effects.

4 **Flashbacks.**
The plot generally moves readers forward in the story from the **beginning** to the **middle** to the **end**. The events can be presented in the order in which they occur, or sometimes they can be seen through a series of **flashbacks**. When using flashbacks, an author sometimes presents the conflict that a character faces early in the novel and then returns to the beginning of the story line. Novelists may also weave flashbacks throughout the events in a novel in order to lead the reader to a better understanding of the decisions that a character makes.

No matter how the events are presented, readers need to be able to recognize the sequence of events and to determine how the events influence the main character. Readers need to understand:
- why each event occurred; and
- the outcome or result of each event.

TALKING ABOUT PLOT

First identify the main events in the story. Select events from different parts of the novel and talk about the **causes** and the **effects** of the events. Discuss why readers consider the events identified to be significant. Focus on the **problems** the characters face in these events, the **decisions** that the main character makes and identify any **changes** that may have occurred because of the event. Talk about any event that readers feel needed to be more fully developed in order to better understand why the event was included in the story.

Identify events or subplots involving important and minor characters. Give support for how these events contributed to the main character's actions and choices, even though the main character may not have participated in the event. Discuss why the author may have included these events and what the reader was able to learn about the main character from minor events and subplots. Talk about how the events and subplots enhanced or detracted from the story.

Describe an event in the story where a character exhibited a strong feeling or reaction. Share perceptions of how the character felt or reacted and how the causes and effects of this event contributed to the story line. Readers might also want to talk about events in the story to which they had strong reactions.

Share any surprises readers encountered in the events in the story line. Talk about how these surprises differed from what readers predicted was going to happen. Readers may also want to share why specific events from the novel were enjoyable or memorable.

When readers make personal connections to an event in the story, have them talk about their personal experiences and compare the causes and effects of these personal events with the ones that occurred in the novel. Readers might also want to share the effect of an event on them and compare how the outcome was alike or different from what happened to the characters in the novel.

Talk about an event from another novel that was similar to something that happened in the novel being discussed. Compare causes and effects of the events and discuss what the characters in both novels learned from the experiences.

Share opinions about the author's skill in developing the plot by discussing the sequence in which the events were presented. Decide if the story was presented in a clear, orderly and understandable manner. If the author uses flashbacks, discuss the effectiveness of their use and if the flashbacks added to or detracted from the plot. Determine if the author included enough or too much information. Talk about how readers connected to the plot and if the author was able to maintain the readers' desire to continue to read.

SEE PAGE 28 FOR SUGGESTED DISCUSSION QUESTIONS ABOUT PLOT.

CHARACTERISTIC: CONFLICT/RESOLUTION

Conflict/resolution concerns the major conflict faced by the main character, the decision the character makes to resolve the conflict and the effectiveness of the character's decision.

1 Conflict.

A conflict is the **struggle** a character experiences when faced with a problem and the **choice** he/she must make between opposing needs, ideas or issues. A conflict always requires that a decision be made or an action be taken to solve a problem or change an unacceptable situation. **For example, a father knows that his son had been involved in an accident. The boy was at fault but refuses to accept responsibility. The father's conflict is that, knowing there will be significant family consequences if the truth is told, he has to decide whether or not to support the son's decision.**

A conflict is essential to every novel. Characters face problems and experience situations that lead to a conflict. Throughout a novel, an author attempts to present everything that the reader needs to know. An author creates tension and pressure until, near the end of the story, the conflict needs to be resolved. Readers can recognize the conflict when the main character experiences increased tension and must make an important decision about how to resolve the tension. One way to identify the conflict is to recognize the point in the novel when the main character says or thinks, "On the one hand I could do this; on the other hand I could do that." The reader focuses on the choices the character has to make in order to answer this question and on how the character acts in a situation that will have an effect on the character's life, activities or future.

Conflicts can be internal (personal) or external (reactions to the world).

Examples of conflicts generally found in novels include:
- conflicts related to interactions with another individual: friend, family member, enemy, etc.;
- conflicts related to groups of people: other cultures, other political points of view, other belief systems, etc.;
- conflicts related to personal development: personal tragedy, physical challenges, age;
- conflicts related to an animal or animals: pet research;
- conflicts related to nature or the natural elements: survival, challenges; and/or
- conflicts related to supernatural forces: aliens, advanced uses of technology.

2 Resolution.

The point in a story when the main character finally decides how to **handle** the conflict is called the **resolution**. Readers identify the resolution by identifying the choice the character makes or plans to make to solve, circumvent or surmount the conflict. **A character decides to emigrate to a new country despite the fact that he will have to leave all of his family and friends behind. A different character decides not to disclose information because of the negative impact she believes the disclosure would have on her family.**

Authors sometimes tell readers whether or not a character's decision was effective in resolving a conflict by including the consequences of the resolution in the story. Readers sometimes have to predict the effectiveness of the resolution and the effect of the resolution on the character's personality and future actions.

Talking About Conflict/Resolution

First, identify the conflict and the way in which it was resolved. Novels usually parallel real life situations, therefore, the conflicts and resolutions are often similar to experiences faced by readers or their acquaintances.

Discuss personal conflicts that readers have experienced that are similar to those of the characters in the novel. Sometimes, a character's conflict provides readers with the opportunity to consider problems and situations totally alien to their own experiences. This might be interesting to talk about.

Talk about the main character's conflict and the way in which this character resolved or planned to resolve the conflict. Discuss if readers agree or disagree with the character's decision.

Discuss the events and interactions that led to the conflict. Talk about which minor characters represented different points of view and contributed to the stress and pressure.

Discuss the choices the character makes and hypothesize about how the readers might have resolved the conflict in a similar situation. Compare ways readers predict the character might behave in future situations.

Identify the type of conflict in the story and support the choice by referring to specific information from the story. Compare the type of conflict in the novel with the same type of conflict in a different story. Also, compare how different characters resolve similar conflicts.

Give opinions about the effectiveness of a character's decision or offer suggestions of other possibilities the character might have considered. Discuss advice that readers would offer the character.

Share what readers have learned from an experience in the novel and how readers might use this knowledge in a future situation.

SEE PAGE 29 FOR SUGGESTED DISCUSSION QUESTIONS ABOUT CONFLICT/RESOLUTION.

CHARACTERISTIC: CHARACTER MOTIVATION

Character motivation concerns the intent of characters' behaviors and decisions.

Character motivation relates to the **purpose** behind a character's behaviors and to the **reasons** that characters behave and make their decisions in given ways. Characters behave in certain ways in an effort to meet their needs. **For example, a character might steal bread in order to feed his starving family. A different character might steal bread because he feels that society has not treated him fairly and he is not willing to work to survive.**

In order to fully understand a character's motivation, actions and choices, readers try to determine the **intent** of the character's behavior. A writer can only include a limited amount of information in any one text, and this must provide readers with enough background information about the character's family history, descriptions of past relationships and experiences for readers to understand the character's intents. **Does the character act out because a parent treated the character abusively? Does the character become obsessed with work and success despite the effect it has on relationships because the character came from a poor family and fears he will be unable to support his family? Does the character become a human rights activist because her** family lived in a location where individuals were punished if they expressed views different from those of the government in power?

Character motivation is different from characterization. **Characterization** relates to understanding **how** a character behaves, a character's traits, feelings and attitudes. **Character motivation** concerns identifying and understanding the **reasons** that a character's traits, feelings and attitudes developed in the first place and what drives the character as a result.

A character's intent can be positive or negative. Examples of **positive intents** include the desire:

- to survive;
- to improve a situation or behavior;
- to make oneself or others feel good or better;
- to protect a person, animal, country, etc.;
- to persuade or convince oneself or another to behave in a positive manner;
- to acknowledge responsibility;
- to avoid harm; and/or
- to teach.

Examples of **negative intents** include the desire:
- to deceive or trick;
- to punish or harm;
- to profit at someone's expense;
- to avenge a situation through revenge; and/or
- to avoid taking responsibility.

TALKING ABOUT CHARACTER MOTIVATION

First, identify actions or behaviors that occurred in specific situations and share readers' perceptions of the characters' intents. Talk about what the characters said, thought or did and why readers feel the characters might have behaved in a particular way. Talk about readers' perceptions of a character's intent and give information from the story that helped readers understand that character's intent. It can be exciting when group members disagree about the intent of a character's actions.

Consider a reaction, decision or choice a character made and talk about the character's intent in this situation. Discuss if the character's decision was positively or negatively motivated in this specific situation. Talk about whether the author included enough information for the reader and identify what additional details readers needed to better understand the character's intent or motivation for a particular action.

Consider the main character's overall behavior in the novel. Talk about what may have contributed to the character's personality by discussing what readers know about the character's background of experience and personal relationships. Speculate about what might have happened differently in the story if the character's background of experience had been different. Have readers share opinions about how skillful the author was in helping the reader understand why the character behaved in the way he/she did.

Characters in novels are often faced with situations and opportunities similar to those presented to individuals in real life and to characters described in other novels. Talk about these similar situations and share what readers feel motivated them or other characters to behave in the ways they did. Because readers are so diverse and have such different backgrounds and life experiences, discussions about character motivation are often interesting and lead readers to new insights about themselves.

SEE PAGE 30 FOR SUGGESTED DISCUSSION QUESTIONS ABOUT CHARACTER MOTIVATION.

THEME

Theme concerns an author's attempt to offer lessons or universal truths about the world and human experience through the content of a story. The theme is the **central idea**, the **lesson** or the **point** that an author has infused throughout the entire novel and wants the reader to consider or learn.

A novelist sometimes tries to teach readers a lesson or to make a personal point about a problem or issue through a fictional experience. A theme is seldom stated directly. Readers infer the theme by analyzing the five characteristics of the novel and by looking for a pattern to emerge from the story. **An author might focus on the effect of setting to show that people can survive and function in any type of physical environment. A character's willingness or unwillingness to change might suggest the impact of narrow thinking on the battles that individuals have with themselves and others. The effectiveness of an unexpected decision that a character makes after a significant experience might represent an author's attitude that through change people can learn to live in peace and harmony.** An author attempts to include enough information so that a reader can infer a message or the lesson intended.

An author has specific reasons for including each event in the novel or for revealing specific information about a character's personality and background of experience. An author might include certain events or reveal specific information in order to convince readers to consider a particular moral attitude. At the end of a novel, readers are often able to apply characters' decisions and insights to their own lives or to reaffirm personal attitudes or points of view. Through the development of a theme, authors often motivate readers to think about people, cultures, moral principles and social ideas in new and different ways.

Examples of themes often included in novels:
* people are able to readjust to life after bad things happen;
* it is important for individuals to strive actively for good to triumph over evil;
* people should value friendship above all other relationships;
* when people guess at the motives of others, they are often wrong;
* some ideas are worth fighting for despite the consequences to the individual; and/or
* adults can learn important lessons from children.

When developing a theme, authors often use characters, objects and events as symbols that represent the human condition and/or principles and ideas. Authors sometimes present characters that take on heroic qualities in order to represent human values.

Talking About Theme

Because the theme of a novel is seldom stated explicitly, discussions about theme are often highly stimulating and often lead group members to new insights about the novel, about themselves and about the world in general. Talk about what readers propose as the theme — the message or the lesson of the novel. Offer support from the novel for each reader's proposal.

Talk about single words or a short phrase that could be used to identify the topic that the theme relates to (loneliness, responsibility, friendship, etc.). Support why that one word can be used to summarize the main idea of the novel. Have readers come up with a sentence that describes the topic and talk about how the novel represents this message.

Discuss how the author used each of the five characteristics of the novel (setting, characterization, plot, conflict/resolution, character motivation) to lead readers to the theme. Talk about how the conflict the main character faces relates to the theme and identify the roles played by other characters.

Once the theme has been identified, talk about additional events or actions the author might have included or events that could have been omitted. Discuss the roles played by characters in the story. Discuss if characters, objects or events were used as symbols for abstract ideas.

Describe a real life event or experience that illustrates the theme represented in the novel. Readers might also compare the theme in the novel with the way the same idea was presented in another story. Share an insight about people or relationships that a reader may never have considered before. Discuss insights readers gained about themselves that relate to the theme. Talk about how the message might be extended to apply to current social, cultural and/or world situations.

Readers can share opinions about the author's skill in developing the theme. Decide if the author was able to convey a message or lesson without being obvious or preachy. Share whether or not readers agree with the author's message and have readers give reasons for their positions.

SEE PAGE 31 FOR SUGGESTED DISCUSSION QUESTIONS ABOUT THEME.

SUGGESTED QUESTIONS TO ASK

Even though all five characteristics of a novel are present in every story, in a discussion one characteristic may require more focus. Each characteristic can be drawn out by a different type of question. Questions do not have to be discussed in a specific order; one discussion might start with a focus on setting and another with a focus on plot. It is not necessary to ask questions about each story characteristic. The goal in planning for a discussion is to select those questions that will lead to an in-depth discussion.

WHEN TALKING ABOUT BOOKS

Questions That Lead to Talking About Setting

1 How significant is the setting in this novel?

2 How does the time period affect the characters' decisions?

3 How does the place in which the story occurs affect the characters' decisions?

4 What effect, if any, does the setting have on the events or characters in the story?

5 If you are familiar with or have read about this setting, how does the author's presentation compare with your experience?

6 Have you read other novels set in this place and time? How does the setting in this novel compare?

7 Was there enough description of the setting to provide a backdrop for the characters?

8 Did the author's description of the setting add to your enjoyment of the novel? Why or why not?

9 At what points in the story would you have liked the author to have given more detail about the setting?

10 How might the people, events and actions in the story have been effected if the story had been set in a different time or place?

11 What was a specific image of the setting that you enjoyed? Why did this image appeal to you?

12 Where is the author of this novel from? How might the author's background have influenced the setting that is described?

13 Since this novel is set in the past, what insights about the effect of living at that time did you gain?

14 Since this novel is set in the future, what insights about the effect of living in the future did you gain?

15 Is the setting in this story more important than the characters and/or the events? Why or why not?

Questions That Lead to Talking About Characterization

1 Who is the main character in this novel? Why do you think so?

2 What traits would you use to describe the main character? What are some behaviors that illustrate those traits?

3 What are some feelings the characters experienced? What are the reasons for these feelings?

4 Does the main character have an attitude about a person, event, or issue? How would you describe the character's attitude?

5 What are some feelings you had about one of the characters in the story? Their traits? Feelings? Attitudes?

6 How are any of the character's traits, feelings or attitudes in this story like or different from those of people you know?

7 How does the main character in this novel compare to a character in another book you have read? A person you know?

8 What are the roles played by significant and minor characters in the novel?

9 Has the author stereotyped any of the characters? How?

10 Describe something about a character that you admired.

11 Describe something about a character that you did not admire.

12 Share an insight you gained about yourself as you were reading about a character in this novel?

13 What is the author's attitude toward the characters in this book?

14 Predict how a character will behave or feel after the story ends. Give reasons for your prediction.

15 What additional information would you like to have had about the characters in this story in order to understand them better?

Questions That Lead to Talking About Plot

1 What is the main event in this story? Why do you consider it to be a main event? What are the causes of the event? What are the outcomes?

2 What are some of the decisions that the main character makes in relation to an event in this novel?

3 Describe an event in the story where a character exhibits a strong feeling or reaction. How does the character feel and how does the event affect the character?

4 Identify an event in the novel that caused you to strongly react. Why?

5 What is an event in the novel that needs to be more fully developed in order for you to have a better understanding of this story?

6 Describe an event from the story that is similar to something that happened in another novel you have read. How are the events the same? How are they different?

7 Describe a personal connection you had with an event in the novel.

8 What is an event in the story that you would like to know more about?

9 Are there any events in the story that you find confusing? What might the author have done differently to clear up the confusion?

10 What does the main character learn from an event in this novel?

11 What event in the novel is your favorite or the most memorable? Why?

12 Does the author include any subplots? Do they enhance or detract from the story?

13 How skillfully does the author develop the story line?

14 Does the author's skill in presenting events enhance or detract from the story?

15 How successful is the author in using flashbacks?

QUESTIONS THAT LEAD TO TALKING ABOUT CONFLICT/RESOLUTION

1 What are some problems that characters in the novel face?

2 What is the major problem facing the main character?

3 How does the main character resolve his/her conflict?

4 Do you believe the choice the main character makes resolves the conflict effectively?

5 How does the way in which the main character resolves the conflict compare to how you may have behaved in the same situation?

6 Did you learn anything from the way the character resolved his/her conflict that you could use in your own life?

7 Compare a conflict in the novel with a similar conflict that you or someone you know has experienced.

8 Since the effectiveness of the character's resolution is not stated, predict what you feel happened.

9 Do you agree or disagree with the way the character resolves the conflict? Why?

10 What are some other actions the main character might have taken in order to resolve the conflict?

11 What do you feel might have happened if the main character had chosen to resolve the conflict in a different way?

12 Describe a feeling you had about yourself as you were reading about the decision that the main character was making.

13 What advice would you give to one of the characters in the novel?

14 What type of universal conflict does the character's struggle represent?

QUESTIONS THAT LEAD TO TALKING ABOUT CHARACTER MOTIVATION

1 Identify an event or situation in the story and describe how the character behaves. What is the character's intent in behaving the way he/she does?

2 Identify a decision or choice a character makes. What information in the novel contributes to your knowing why the character makes that choice?

3 Identify a situation in the story and describe how another character referred to in the story contributes to the way a certain character behaves.

4 Consider a reaction, decision or choice a character makes. What additional details or information would you like to have in order to better understand the character's intent or motivation for that particular action?

5 Would you describe the actions of the main character to be positively or negatively motivated? Why?

6 What are some of the needs that the characters attempt to satisfy in the novel?

7 What people or events impact the ways in which the characters behave?

8 Describe some of the characters' actions that portray a positive intent. Why do these characters behave positively?

9 Describe some of the characters' actions that portray a negative intent. Why do these characters behave negatively?

10 How effective is the author in helping the reader understand each character's motivation?

11 How do minor characters help the reader understand the main character's motivation for actions and decisions?

12 Have you ever behaved in a way similar to the main character? What motivated you to do so?

13 Characters in different novels are often faced with the same opportunities. Can you think of a character in a different novel who behaves differently in the same type of situation? Why?

14 What additional information would you like to have in order to better understand a character's intent or motivation for a particular behavior?

Questions That Lead to Talking About Theme

1 What is the theme represented in the novel? What evidence from the novel supports this theme?

2 Does the novel have a message? What does the author want the reader to learn from the story?

3 What did you learn from the theme presented in the novel about people or relationships that you had never considered before?

4 What is a key word that you could use to summarize the theme of the novel?

5 Describe a part of the novel that contributes to the development of the theme.

6 How are the five characteristics of a novel used to develop a lesson or message?

7 Describe a real life event or experience that illustrates the theme represented in the novel.

8 What is an insight you gained about yourself that relates to the theme of the novel?

9 Have you read a different novel with a similar theme?

10 Do you agree or disagree with the author's message in the novel? Why?

11 What else might the author have included in the story to better illustrate or develop the theme?

12 What actions or events in the novel best illustrate the theme?

13 How skillful is the author in leading the reader to the theme?

14 Which of the characters or objects in the novel are used symbolically?

GUIDELINES FOR BOOK DISCUSSION GROUP MEETINGS

Careful planning for the first meeting contributes to maintaining the group, and adds to the early success of a book discussion group.

Reviewing possible group member roles, the logistics of getting together and the suggested ground rules for discussions can help group members reach a consensus as to what they want their group to be.

Preparing for the First Book Discussion Group Meeting

1 After members have been identified, take time to agree on the date, location, time and title for the first discussion. Discussion groups generally meet one time each month for between two and two-and-a-half hours.

2 It is important for all members to have a common reading vocabulary during discussions. If multiple copies of *Talking About Books* are available, have all participants read the guide before the first meeting. If members have not had the opportunity to read *Talking About Books*, take time at the first meeting to review the sections: **"What Happens During a Book Discussion Group Meeting?"** and **"The Five Characteristics and Theme of a Novel."**

3 Discuss group member roles suggested below. Groups may decide to designate one person for each role, or alternate the opportunities among interested members. Suggested group member roles include:

• A **Facilitator** who selects the discussion questions, facilitates the meeting, and makes sure all members have an opportunity to contribute to the discussion.

• A **Secretary/Contact Person** who compiles and distributes member addresses and phone numbers and maintains a list of books that have been read by the group. Some bookstores give discounts for the purchase of multiple copies. If necessary, the secretary can order multiple copies of books.

• A **Refreshments Coordinator** may be identified to supply or order beverages and/or light snacks.

• A designated **Timekeeper** should monitor the clock and ensure that meetings begin and end at the designated time.

4 Creating and maintaining a group notebook of titles read and questions asked provides the group with a history. **"Discussion Planning Sheets,"** included in this guide, can be detached and/or photocopied for your convenience. Completed discussion sheets on each title can be included in the group notebook. Group facilitators can also use the notebook to review questions asked in the past in order to vary the focus and to emphasize different aspects of stories.

5 Always agree on the book to be read as a group. For the first book discussion, if the

group is unable to agree in advance, have the first facilitator choose the book to discuss, inform participants of the title, and select questions from those provided in this guide.

6 Discuss and agree on ground rules for group meetings. Possible ground rules include:
- Come to the discussion group having read the book.
- Begin meetings at the agreed upon time.
- Provide refreshments as agreed.
- Stick to the topic by limiting personal discussions to comments that relate to the book's content.
- Maintain a non-threatening atmosphere by listening first to hear and second to react.
- Agree to disagree in a respectful manner because there are no right or wrong answers.

- Allow everyone the opportunity to participate equitably.
- Come prepared to lead the discussion if you are the designated facilitator.

7 Ask members to think about titles to recommend for future meetings. Proposed titles can be located in newspaper book reviews, bookstores or recommended by friends. Local libraries often provide lists of books organized by topic, author and literary awards. Members should reach consensus about the selections to be read. Consensus means that all participants can live with the decision even though one individual might have preferred that a different novel be chosen. Some groups agree to a schedule for the year; other groups select titles monthly.

At the First Book Discussion Group Meeting

1 Arrange a physical area for discussion by placing chairs in a circle or around a table.

2 When all members have arrived, make introductions and take time to have each member share a bit about themselves.

3 Begin the discussion by having the facilitator ask a prepared question and share a personal response. Ask other members of the group to contribute their thoughts and ideas about the same question.

4 Before concluding the meeting, take time to evaluate the meeting by asking for reactions to the discussion, for commitment to group participation, and for any recommendations about how to make the meeting more successful.

5 Come to consensus about the book title for the next book club meeting. Be sure everyone is in agreement that they want to read the proposed title.

6 Designate the facilitator for the next meeting, as well as changes in other group member roles.

7 Set the date, time and place for the next meeting.

Suggested Book Discussion Group Ground Rules

1   Come to the discussion group having read the book.

2   Begin meetings at the agreed upon time.

3   Agree on if and how refreshments will be provided.

4   Stick to the topic by limiting personal discussions to comments that relate to the book content.

5   Maintain a non-threatening atmosphere by listening first to hear and second to react.

6   Agree to disagree in a respectful manner because there are no right or wrong answers.

7   Allow everyone the opportunity to participate equitably.

8   Come prepared to lead the discussion if you are the designated facilitator.

DISCUSSION PLANNING SHEETS

The discussion planning sheets included in this guide are designed to help book discussion groups prepare to talk about books. Facilitators might choose to ask one question about each of the five characteristics and theme of a novel, or to focus questions only on those characteristics that are most significant to a particular book. Questions do not need to be asked in any specific order, nor do a specific number of questions need to be prepared. Group members can also select questions to ask.

DISCUSSION PLANNING SHEET

Title _____

Author _____ Date _____

DISCUSSION QUESTIONS

Setting _____
_____
_____
_____
_____

Characterization _____
_____
_____
_____
_____

Plot _____
_____
_____
_____
_____

Conflict Resolution _____
_____
_____
_____
_____

Character Motivation _____
_____
_____
_____
_____

Theme _____
_____
_____
_____
_____

DUPLICATION OF THIS DISCUSSION PLANNING SHEET IS PERMITTED.

DISCUSSION PLANNING SHEET

Title _____

Author _____ Date _____

DISCUSSION QUESTIONS

Setting _____
_____
_____
_____
_____

Characterization _____
_____
_____
_____
_____

Plot _____
_____
_____
_____
_____

Conflict Resolution _____
_____
_____
_____
_____

Character Motivation _____
_____
_____
_____
_____

Theme _____
_____
_____
_____
_____

Discussion Planning Sheet

Title _____

Author _____ Date _____

Discussion Questions

S etting _____

_____

_____

_____

_____

C haracterization _____

_____

_____

_____

_____

P lot _____

_____

_____

_____

_____

C onflict Resolution _____

_____

_____

_____

_____

C haracter Motivation _____

_____

_____

_____

_____

T heme _____

_____

_____

_____

_____

Discussion Planning Sheet

Title _____

Author _____ Date _____

Discussion Questions

Setting _____
_____
_____
_____
_____

Characterization _____
_____
_____
_____
_____

Plot _____
_____
_____
_____
_____

Conflict Resolution _____
_____
_____
_____
_____

Character Motivation _____
_____
_____
_____
_____

Theme _____
_____
_____
_____
_____

Discussion Planning Sheet

Title _____

Author _____ Date _____

Discussion Questions

Setting _____
_____
_____
_____
_____

Characterization _____
_____
_____
_____
_____

Plot _____
_____
_____
_____
_____

Conflict Resolution _____
_____
_____
_____
_____

Character Motivation _____
_____
_____
_____
_____

Theme _____
_____
_____
_____
_____

Discussion Planning Sheet

Title _____

Author _____ Date _____

Discussion Questions

Setting _____

_____

_____

_____

_____

Characterization _____

_____

_____

_____

_____

Plot _____

_____

_____

_____

_____

Conflict Resolution _____

_____

_____

_____

_____

Character Motivation _____

_____

_____

_____

_____

Theme _____

_____

_____

_____

_____

DUPLICATION OF THIS DISCUSSION PLANNING SHEET IS PERMITTED.

DISCUSSION PLANNING SHEET

Title _____

Author _____ Date _____

DISCUSSION QUESTIONS

Setting _____
_____
_____
_____
_____

Characterization _____
_____
_____
_____
_____

Plot _____
_____
_____
_____
_____

Conflict Resolution _____
_____
_____
_____
_____

Character Motivation _____
_____
_____
_____
_____

Theme _____
_____
_____
_____
_____

DUPLICATION OF THIS DISCUSSION PLANNING SHEET IS PERMITTED.